A Skeleton Without A Face

Taryn Kliewer

Presentation by *BookLeaf Publishing*

Web: www.bookleafpub.com

E-mail: info@bookleafpub.com

ISBN: 978-93-5744-736-2

First edition 2022

DEDICATION

I want to dedicate this book to someone I used to know for teaching me how to live in the darkness.

Part I: My Last Breath

It's been a year since I tried to end my life. Since I sat on my bedroom floor crying - begging for the pain to go away. Since I downed two bottles of pills and a bottle of alcohol that used to bring fun, only now to bring pain and addiction. It's been a year since my mom rushed me to the hospital after I called to tell her what I had done and to say goodbye. Since my best friend held my hand in the emergency room while I slept, incapable of opening my eyes. Since my lifeless body couldn't tell the doctor what I had done. It's been a year since I spent a horrifying 5 days in a psych unit going through withdrawals. Since I had a breakdown and yelled at every tech and nurse in the unit. Since I begged anyone whose number I had to come get me out of that hell. It's been a year since I sat alone in my room without anything to do except dissipate into someone who no longer exists. Since I sat alone in the darkness. Since the only thing I had was the bottle of jack and the bottle of benzos next to

me. It's been a year since my last breath
would've been such a happy ending.

Addiction

The sadness pours from my eyes like a waterfall
fleeing to the bottom of a cold, rocky cliff.
My lips tingle as I cry at the girl in the mirror.
The skeleton looking at me is not human.
My hands tremble, and my face turns white
while the shame runs up my throat.
The guilt will stop at nothing to burn down
what's left of me.
My lungs are trapped inside a cage that keeps
growing smaller and smaller.
I can't breathe.
Shrink my body into oblivion.
Lose the person I used to be.
Why does my source of survival kill me rather
than keep me alive?
Why do I feel proud when my stomach rumbles
like a thunderstorm?
Why have I never felt so alive than when I
crumble to the floor like something I'd only
pretend to eat?
The pain never ends.
I'm shattered glass waiting to be cut with the
broken pieces.

The only thing I want is to disappear into the
addiction that started with just wanting to be a
little smaller, a little more unseen.
I can't stop.
My mind is frantic.
The voice tells me to go one more day,
Make it one more day and you'll disappear.
Just don't swallow the thing that kills.
Chew up your words and spit them out like they
were never ingested.
Call me out on my bullshit.
Save me.
Take me to the light.
Take me to the other side where I can finally see
color again.
Blush will return to my cheeks.
My eyes will light up again.
My legs will carry me to the outdoors where I
can play in the rain without crying.
My fingers will write like they were never
shoved down my throat.
My body will move and dance like it was never
a skeleton without a face.
But the darkness sucks me in.
Its too attractive to let go.
It lures me in deeper and deeper until there's
nothing left of me except a bitter bag of bones.

My Suicide Note

Why am I so afraid of death? Why am I afraid of nothingness-the end of all inevitable and incurable darkness that consumes my mind? My whole life I've waited for better days. I've sat alone in my room for nights on end and begged for death. Something that would be a little easier on those I love. Instead, I've resorted to the bottle of pills in my drawer that scream my name. They scream empty promises for an end that's much brighter. I've resorted to the alcohol that sits on the bottom shelf in the fridge. I've resorted to laying in my bed and taking my last breath. At least this way I won't be succumbed into the storm that rips apart my mind. If you're reading this, it means you've found me. It means you've found me finally at peace - finally myself. No more hurting. No more darkness, and no more longing for a life I'll never have.

Reality

I hold her hand while she sits next to me. She kisses me gently and whispers sweet nothings in my ear. Her breath gives me chills and her words slither in my ear like a serpent telling you a secret. Her eyes wrap around me, giving me a hug. Her eyelashes flutter against my skin like a small butterfly,. Her mouth opens to gawk at me while her lies whisper yet another. Her hair succumbs me into warmth. With each strand, I fall deeper and deeper. Her hand runs up my thigh and tickles my skin with her delicate and welcoming fingertips. Her arms reach out to embrace me, but then I notice a change in her face.

The wind starts to blow. The thunder starts to yell. Her voice grows louder and louder. Her spine cracks and her veins and nerves pour everywhere. She is turning into who I am on the inside. Her eyes glow red, and she becomes a snake. Her words creep into my ears and her eyes burn my skin. Her whispers of sweet nothings have turned into intrusive thoughts. The aura around her shifts into punishment. Her breath grows fierce with the winds, and her cry yells out with the thunder. Her hands grasp my

neck and pulls the breath out of me. She jumps
to her feet and pulls me up with her. The wind
tears me apart. My eyes melt out of my face, and
my skin turns scaly. My fingertips sprout out
claws and my feet turn cold.
Her embrace seems familiar. My eyes bat open.
I'm out of breath. Who is she? What does she
want from me? It frightens me how familiar her
touch is. It almost soothes me. It comforts me. It
keeps me wanting to know more in hopes I'll get
to meet her again. Who is she? "Death", she
replies. "I have finally come to get you".

Pain

Pain.
It's just a four letter word.

Pain is the feeling you get when you glide the razor across your leg for the fourth time this week. It's what you feel when the blood drips down onto the shower floor. It's when you feel release with every brutal mark you make to your skin. It's seeing the art you've created. It's feeling better after causing more physical torture than mental. But that isn't pain... right?

Pain is the feeling you get when your "best friend" gets you drunk and touches your body in ways that's only meant to be touched with passion rather than aggression. It's the feeling you get when they enter the part of your body that was only made for love, not for fucking. It's what you feel when his hand explores your body with no intention of being gentle. It's what you feel when he goes harder and faster, removing any feeling of self respect and self love that was never even there to begin with. His lips suck the life out of your already broken body. His eyes

wonder and go places they don't belong. His fingers aggressively trace every inch of your body while you internally scream for help, but your mouth can't form any words because the alcohol is too overbearing. It's the feeling you get when you lay there naked and let him have his way with you.
But that isn't pain... right?

Pain is the feeling you get when you swallow another pill out of the bottle that controls you more than you control it. It whispers your name every time you walk into your room. The pill turns your mind into a whirlwind with every one you swallow. It tingles your body. It's your escape. It's the reason you push forward. But that isn't pain... right?

Pain is the feeling you get when you've eaten over 500 calories in one day. It's the feeling you get when your stomach yells at you, but you only give it celery for the 7th time today.
It's what you feel when your body is constantly cold because it is deprived of the warmth and comfort from your favorite meal that you haven't eaten in months. It's when your body is so exhausted that you almost pass out at work. It's when your friends compliment your weight loss which only triggers you to go a step further

with your obsession. You run everywhere. You
weigh yourself 10 times a day. You don't go out
in public because you feel fat. You don't go out
with your friends and enjoy milkshakes or go to
the movies because milkshakes have too many
calories and your friends will hear your stomach
growl in the theater. It's the feeling you get
when you're fighting for survival with every
pound you lose. But that isn't pain... right?

Pain is the feeling you get when you sit in your
room all alone at 2 in the morning with nothing
on your mind except for the four walls that
surround you. It's what you get when the
darkness in the room takes over any light you
thought you had. It's what you get when you
haven't left your room in 4 days. It's the feeling
you get when your mom sobs in front of you as
you lay on the floor in a puddle of your own
tears from crying about your suicide attempt not
working yet again. It's the feeling you get when
suicide is your favorite thing to think about. It's
what you get when your body starts to float
because you're so incapable of reality. You float
to the ceiling and look down at your lifeless
body in hopes that you can finally disappear.
You watch your lover and your sister and your
mom stare at your cold face and your defunct
body. It's the feeling you get when you are

sucked back in only to wake up and face another day of pain and misery. But that isn't pain... right?

Pain? It's the four letter word that your darkness hides behind.

Broken Mirrors

Opening a bottle of pills is an antidote for the darkness I've been stuck in. The hallucinations make me see what my mind is really thinking and feeling. I can reach out and touch my tears. I can touch my tombstone. "Here lies the girl who was once consumed with darkness but has now been consumed by death" I can touch my scars like they're not on my body. It helps me slip away while I stare at the girl in the broken mirror. My eyes vibrate and spin from the high I get. I can see myself from a different perspective. I grab pieces of broken glass and slowly glide them down my thighs and my shoulders and my stomach and everywhere else just like it was a natural thing to do. I see myself sitting on the floor with my hands covered in blood and a puddle of tears beneath me. My hair weeps along with me, begging to stay, to help me hide, but it's falling to the floor with every clump I yank from my scalp. The pain... it's euphoric. I'm ripping myself away while everyone else wants to fix me. Why can't I just break apart in peace? The feeling of blood dripping down my body makes me feel warm. I slice all over my body just screaming and inviting all of that darkness in. My hair is wet from the sweat pouring out of my skin. I'm naked. I'm naked and sitting on the bathroom floor praying to whomever is out there to take me away. To let me have my last breath. To finally give me peace.

Demons

I need you to know that I love you. I need you to know that my heart is heavy with so much of nothing. I can't feel anything. I can't feel sadness. I can't feel anger. I can't feel joy. I can't feel love. I'm sorry if I've been distant lately. I know that love is somewhere deep inside of me, I just can't get it to resurface. My emotions are all over the place yet going no where at all. I'm covered in fire that burns my skin every time I get out of bed. It's getting harder to breathe. My mind is an ocean of thoughts, except they're all drowning. I try to come up for air, but my demons push me back down underwater.

I Want There To Be Nothing

I'm just at a total loss right now. I can't eat. I can barely breathe. It feels like I'm at war when I go to work. The only time I feel okay is when I'm sleeping or cuddling my cats. The world is constantly jumping in circles around me - making me dizzy, numb, isolated, can't catch my breath. I can't see anything or anyone. I'm in a bubble surrounded by people who pretend to care or pretend to want to help but are blind to what's on the inside.
I'm stuck in a hurricane with everything blowing against my face, blinding me from seeing reality. What am I even doing here? It's not like I actually exist. Nothing is going my way. No one wants me. I've bounced back and forth between places to live for the past 5 months. It's absolutely exhausting. I can't catch a break. Every time I try to settle and calm myself and try to get my shit together, my life uproots, and I have to start all over again… it's unbearable. Yesterday morning I took a handful of sleeping

pills to try to escape reality. I didn't care what the consequences would be. In that moment, I just wanted to cease to exist. So I slept. I slept until my alarm went off for me to get ready for work.

I lied. I didn't really have a headache. I mean, I did but only because the darkness was so overbearing that it hurt. So I called out. I called out and slept again for a long time. It still wasn't enough. I just don't know where I am or who I am, and I know, trust me, I've been told by multiple people that everyone feels this way at some point, but what if this is all I've ever felt? I'm tired of people telling me that my feelings are normal. I'm so sick of people telling me that it'll be okay. I'm so sick of people not believing what goes on in my head. I'm so sick of people telling me to think of the positives. I'm so sick of people giving me advice about something they know nothing of. Everyone's experience of the darkness is different so don't fucking compare to mine. I'm so sick of people telling me things that I've always thought of, and since I've done those things, don't you think I'd be better if they worked? I'm so sick of life. What if there isn't a way out or a plan to work itself out? What if I'm alone? What if I'm just on this never ending cycle of pain? What if everyday is one day closer to me finally just ending myself?

I want peace. I want silence. I want there to be nothing.

A Skeleton Without A Face

I miss you today.
I miss your droopy brown eyes surrounded by
visibly cut orbital bones.
I miss your pale blue lips when you're cold,
which, let's face it, you're cold the majority of
the time.
I miss your smile: the one where you can tell
you're broken, but your cracked lips force open
anyways.
I miss your raspy voice: the one where you can
tell you haven't slept in days, but you manage to
make sounds anyways.
I miss your hair: the brittleness caused by an
illness that won't go away.
I miss your skin: cold to the touch, excess hair in
attempt for warmth.
I miss your body: the fragility of all your bones
rising beneath the surface. The way your collar
bones dipped in at your neck, forming a perfect
place for a little pond. Your hips and the way
their bones would hide beneath your clothes.

Your legs and the way they carefully tip toed
around, reluctant to be seen. Your cheeks and the
color running away from them. Your fingernails
chipping away with every touch. Your spine and
the way it runs down your body getting closer to
the surface.

I miss you. I miss the days we could starve
together. The days we could drink some apple
juice and call it a day. The days we would do
squats and lift dumbbells in hot weather. I miss
the days our heads would get so high from the
emptiness that we would fall over. The days
where people would compliment how good we
looked, how hard they could tell we were
working. I miss looking in the mirror and seeing
a skeleton without a face.

I Wish You Would Notice Me

You're sitting next to me, yet I've never felt so
far away from you.
I hear you breathing, but I also hear you
withering away.
Your eyes hold so much sadness.
Your skin holds a lot of pain.
Every scar yells in agony because it wishes to
have you back.
Your smile weakens as the day goes by.
I see you laying in bed only you're not really
there.
I hold your hand, but I can't feel you.
I hear you talk, but no words come out.
Your soul holds so much dejection.
It's weak.
It's pale.
It's hollow.
You kiss me but I only feel a small sensation
because you're barely even there.
We make love yet it's just a distant memory.
I lay in bed and cry over how much I wish you
would hold me in your arms.

I crave your embrace.
I crave your touch.
I crave your love.
I crave being yours.
Well,
I am yours, but sometimes it feels as though you
slip away, and I feel like you don't want me
anymore.
You've seen my insanity.
You've seen my pain.
You've seen my anger.
You've witnessed my nightmares, a nightmare in
which I'm the nightmare.
I stare at the ceiling and dream of us dancing
together.
I wish you would tell me you love me with more
than just your words.
I wish you would acknowledge when I speak.
I wish you would listen.
I wish you would just be present.
I wish you would understand how much pain
I'm in.
I wish you understood how hard I'm trying.
How fast I'm running to catch you.
To make you fall back in love with me.
I dream of you touching me.
I dream of you calling my name.
I dream of you loving me.

You're sitting next to me, yet I've never felt so
far away from you.
I see you sitting next to me, laughing and
smiling at your phone.
I wish you laughed and smiled at me like that...
I see your body resisting me.
I see your body move, yet you're so still.
I see every curve of your body.
I only wish you knew how much I adore you.
I wish you knew how perfect you are to me.
I wish you knew that I love you with my whole
heart.
I wish you knew that if I'm not what you want...
I'll be okay with that.
If I'm too much for you
If I'm too scary
If I'm too angry
If I'm too sad
If I'm too selfish
If I'm too insecure
If I'm too needy
If I'm too clingy
If I'm too demanding
If I'm too sexual
If I'm too damaged
If I'm too boring
If I'm too late to get your attention...
I will understand.

I will understand because I'm too much of those
things for myself.
I can't handle myself.
I'm stupid
I'm reckless
I'm jealous
I'm uncomfortable
I'm overbearing
I know, Taryn.
I know that I'm all of these things.
But you know what?
Despite everything,
I know I love you.
I love you with every ounce of my body.
I love you so much that all I wish for you is
happiness.
But it's okay for you to leave.
Because then you'll be sitting next to me, but I'll
only see it when I look in the mirror.

Naked

I opened the bottle again tonight.
Popped the tab on a can of beer.
Took a blade to my legs.

I looked in the mirror and saw my empty body.
Tipsy, high, bloody.

I picked up the phone to call for help, but my
body froze. I couldn't get my hand to move.

I took my clothes off and laid naked in the floor.
My legs a mess. My mind crazed from the high.
Tipsy because I love to take risks.
I see the woman who was once Taryn. She
smiles at me and tries to comfort me but quickly
dissipates in the blink of an eye. Her presence
lingers. So close I can almost touch it. So strong
that I can smell it. So desirable I can almost taste
it. But no matter how close she gets, my body
freezes solid.

My cold body lays on the floor, shivering,
gasping for air, hopeless, defeated, dark...

Imagination

You know that feeling when you're laying on the floor with your heart beating fast and your breath is short and your vision starts to get blurry and sound starts to go out and you can't feel your body and your mind gets really foggy and you begin to slip away and you finally let out a sigh of relief before you fall asleep? That's how I imagine suicide to be.

Weathering

Weathering the sky is the only escape from the
storm within my mind.
Standing in the rain hurls me into the darkness.
It takes the waters I absorb and shares it with the
ground.
The glum up above envies how dark I can be.
They envy the lightning I'm able to bury in my
scars.
The floor soaks up my tears while I sit and
question whether I should wake up tomorrow.

Part II: A Lover In The Darkness

Even though you were the absolute worst thing that has ever happened to me, I will always love you.

I will love you on a rainy, Sunday morning.

I will love you when I'm taking a shower late at night, and the water reminds me of you gently touching my skin.

I will love you when I hear our song.

I will love you when I'm on long car rides with my best friend in the middle of the day.

I will love you when I'm working at my dream job.

I will love you even when I hate you.

I will love you even when I remember all that you did to me.

I'll remember all the lies.

The sneaking around

The manipulation

You had me begging for your attention.

You knew I was wrapped around your finger.

You knew I was one call away to make love to you even when you just wanted to fuck.

I'd touch you
Kiss you
Feel you with such a passion that no one else
could've given you.
Yet
You'd use me
Chew me up
Spit me out
Over
And over
And over again.

Home

There are days where I long to visit my childhood home, to pull in the driveway and see all the trees surrounding the pavement that my dad did which runs in a circle because I'd like to ride my bike and roller blade with my brother. I see myself sitting on the front porch, rocking on the little white rocking chair that my dad and I used to sit on late at night. I see the stained glass door with rose petals and vines and a golden handle. I walk into the living room and instantly breathe in the air that brought me to life as a child. The red living room walls succumb me into the memories of nights I'd dance in the living room with my daddy. He and mom would dance, and I loved to watch their eyes beam at each other with the kind of love I hoped to have someday. Daddy would take my hand and spin me around and teach me how to dance like he and mom did. We'd turn up the radio late at night, turn on the fireplace, and dance. We'd just dance.

I walk into the kitchen to see the creamy white tile on the floor. I see the rooster backsplash we had around the counters. It was an odd thing to have in the kitchen, but I guess it was humorous.

I'd see the stove where my parents would cook meals that brought so much warmth to my little tummy. I walk onto the back porch and smell the grill that my daddy used all the time. I look out into the backyard to see the little playground we had with the swings and a monstrous slide. Well, it was monstrous to 6 year old me. I go back inside and walk to my bedroom where the walls were purple and decorated with tinker bell borders and stickers. I wanted to fly and be a fairy so badly. I would stay up late into the night and pray to god that I would wake up with the ability to fly.

I lay on the floor and close my eyes, soaking in the soft white light from the ceiling. I run my hands over the beige carpet and feel the soft fibers between my fingers. I open my eyes and look at the ceiling, still pretending that the texture bumps were stars. I close my eyes and replay every memory I have of that bedroom, summers of endless slumber parties, playing with toys, and bursts of laughter with my friends. I go back out onto the front porch and just stand there. I stand there with my eyes closed and recall the last time this home brought me joy. The last thing I can remember is my daddy playing banjo for me. He was so good. His fingers danced so quickly on the strings, and I'd sit in awe of his talent. My daddy would smile at me and keep on playing while I would make up some silly and crazy dance moves. I sit on the steps of the front porch and feel the wind rushing through the trees. The leaves rustle playfully and stammer to the ground. I'll always remember this home. I'll always remember the laughter, the joy, the familiarity… this is my final visit. I had to let it live in order to let it die. I had to visit my home one last time and have one more taste of who I used to be a long, long time ago. I get up and head to my car. I get in, fasten my seatbelt, and drive. I drive away to find my next home, my next adventure. I drive down the interstate blaring my favorite childhood songs and memories and having the ultimate nostalgic extravaganza. I roll the windows down, and I am infinite. I laid to rest the part of my life that changed me. I laid to rest the house that built me. I blink and just for a second, just one little second, I see the happiness I have yet to endure. It's so beautiful. What if this is the final chapter? Well, if it is, I want to make the last page memorable and metamorphic. I want to finally bloom into all the beauty I was planted for. I want to reread it and be in awe of who I've become since that time. I want to write my story and share it with others. I want to show the world that sometimes there are happy endings. Is this the end though? I guess there's only one way to find out…

Our Brilliant Last Bow

Thinking of you is like revisiting my childhood home. I reminisce and seek what built me. I seek the songs that changed my life. I seek the familiarity of your hand in mine. I seek the resistance to visit home and unpack. You say that you're not my home anymore, but you most definitely are. You're my childhood home. You built me. You laid the foundation and you scoured my soul. You are the driveway I pull into to visit my favorite place. You are the stained glass door that opens for me to revisit who I used to be. You open my eyes to see the burgundy walls that succumbed me into warmth next to the fireplace. You are the fairy who sprinkled me with magic and made my dream of flying come true. You are the carpet fibers I can't let go of. You are the banjo that gave me so much fun and energy to just dance away all of my fears and remind me for just a moment how alive I really am. You are the late night dancing that makes me forget about reality. You are the

rocking chair on the front porch that swings
back and forth with the breeze. You are the trees
that flow with the wind in the front yard. You are
the bags I refuse to unpack because my home is
not mine anymore. You are the peace I feel when
I close the front door after revisiting for the last
time. You are the seatbelt protecting me from
harm as I drive into a new beginning. You are
the music I listen to in the car. You, my love,
made me feel infinite. You made me realize that
life doesn't end with a heartbreak. We can move
forward. We will find our new home. We will
seize the day every morning in preparation for
who we really want to be. And maybe we're
already who we're supposed to be. So, my love,
get your white picket fence with all of your
babies. Let him help you write your next story.
Let him take you on new adventures that you've
never imagined before. Let your soul live. Stand
in the sun and scream. Just scream until you feel
so alive that you are infinite. Scream until
you've let go of everything you're holding onto.
And then, hug yourself for being an
extraordinary mommy. Show your baby who
you are. Show your baby your infinity. And
then, stretch out your hand and feel your baby's
touch and embrace it. Embrace the person you
are and who you will be. Embrace your pain,
your past, your home… find that special place to

spend forever in. You deserve it more than
anyone I know. I will always always always love
you. You are my soulmate. I believe the universe
specially planned for us to cross paths. The
universe knew we needed each other in the most
vulnerable ways possible. I think about you
every single day, and I picture the mornings
we'd dance to Broadway music in the kitchen. I
think about what you gave me. I think about
who I've become because of you. Thank you,
lover, thank you for showing me how to live.
Thank you for bringing me back to life. I love
you always, and I will forever be a home you
can revisit. Our brilliant last bow. Our ending.
Until then…

That's What Loving Her Felt Like

You know that feeling when you're driving
down an old highway at full speed with the
windows rolled down and the stars beaming at
you and the wind pushing your arm back and the
music so loud you can't think of anything else
except for that moment and then there's a
sudden red light and you have to slam on your
brakes making tire marks on the road and the
smell of burnt rubber fills your nose and your
heart is beating so fast you go blind for a
moment, barely stopping without crashing into
the person in front of you?
Yeah.
That's what loving her felt like.
Loving her felt like tires screeching to stop,
panicked, but relieved when you finally come to
a halt.
It felt like the wind pushing my arm away while
I put my hand out of the window.

You know that feeling when there's been a
horrible tornado and lots of thunder and the rain

is flooding the streets while lighting is setting
power poles on fire and the waves are crashing
on the shore because the wind is too strong but
then the wind calms down and the tornado goes
away and the lightning is gone and the thunder is
quieter and the rain stops pouring from the sky
and you're in the eye of the thunderstorm?
Yeah.
That's what loving her felt like.

Love Is Anywhere I'm With You

You asked what love feels like for me. The truth? There really aren't many words to describe the kind of love I had that so few are lucky to have, but if I had to describe it, it would be this:

Love is driving down back roads with the windows down and the radio turned all the way up and the wind blowing back your hair.
Love is listening to your favorite song and dancing in the rain.
Love is smelling a warm apple pie at Christmas.
Love is seeing the stars for the first time.
Love is noticing how vibrant each color is and how beautiful they are in their own way.
Love is walking down the sidewalk on a summer day holding hands and watching the birds.
Love is laughing at yourself for saying something that's not even funny.
Love is stroking your cheek and kissing your forehead.

Love is cuddling with you at 1 o'clock in the
morning while laughing at our jokes.
Love is missing you so much I'm in pain.
Love is waking up after a nightmare.
Love is watching the moon crawl across the sky.
Love is reading a book on a stormy day.
Love is lying awake at night while the thought
of you races around my mind.
Love is kissing you until my whole body dives
head first into the ocean without a clue when I'll
come up for air.
Love is sitting in a warm bubble bath.
Love is singing without shame.
Love is infinite.
Love is taking your hand.
Love is holding you while you cry.
Love is carrying you to the light.
Love is talking about the future we have
together.
Love is pulling you into my embrace.
Love is creating a safe space for you to feel all
of your emotions comfortably.
Love is wanting to be with you every second of
the day.
Love is wanting you to be the first person I call
when I have exciting news.
Love is making love to you until my body bursts
into flames.

Love is drowning in your eyes and realizing I
never want to come up for air.
Love is letting you see the skeleton without a
face.
Love is anywhere I'm with you.

Until Then…

My love, tell her that I'm no longer in pain. Tell her that I'm on Mt. Cheaha watching the greatest moments of my life. Tell her that she was the absolute best thing I've ever had. Tell her that I'm walking in a field of sunflowers in a bright green dress with my hand stretched out waiting for her. Tell her that I'm warm and that I'm living on the other side in peace. Tell her that she is still my M. Tell her I'll never forget the moment I fell in love with her. We were in the parking lot of civitan park by the lake, sitting in her car, and listening to Atlas: Two by Sleeping at Last. It was during that song that I felt my soul melt into hers. It was in that moment I fell so deeply in love that I knew my heart was complete. It was then that I knew my soul would be bound to hers forever, even if I am gone. Lover, I love you more than I ever thought was possible. I love you more than I love standing at the top of Mt. Cheaha. I love you more than the days we'd dance to music in the kitchen of your old house. I'll miss our love. Imagine me dancing in a field of sunflowers with a big sun hat, bright green dress, and my hand stretched out for you. I'll be waiting for you. I'll be

waiting for the day I can wrap you in my arms
again. Until then, just know that I've already
seen your white picket fence, and it's gorgeous. I
hope to visit sometime. I love you. Goodbye,
lover. I'm free. I'm at peace, and I'm no longer
hurting. Until I see you again...

My Invitation To You

Have you ever wondered what life would be like without depression? Yeah, me too. The truth though? Depression never really goes away. It's stuck with you. The dark thoughts will forever creep into your mind. We can only learn how to manage it and how to cope with it. Our minds belong to the darkness. It's inevitable, but I see you. I know how you're feeling. We can do this. We can fight these demons. We can fight the darkness. We can find something that shines some light in us. We will be able to dance again. We will be able to experience joy and love. We will have our moments that we truly feel alive. Really, and truly alive. The kind of feeling you only get when the world stops spinning for just a moment, and you can finally take a breath and feel the warmth of the sun on your face again. Now is your chance. Don't wait for next week or next month or even next year. Today is your day to be free. Rid yourself of falling into the darkness. Resist the urge to be succumbed into your thoughts. I believe in you. I promise everything will be okay. Please don't give up. We're in this together. Fight for your life. Fight for your freedom. Fight for the happiness you so dearly deserve. Let's fight for our ability to live rather than just surviving. Let's fight to live a life that's worth something. I know I don't know you personally, but I love you. I hope that my story will inspire you to write yours. I hope my story encourages you to share yours because I promise that you will help so many people. Help them to know they're not alone. My name is Taryn, and this is my invitation for you to feel alive.